Helen Steiner Rice

COLLECTION OF
ENCOURAGEMENT

BARBOUR
PUBLISHING

ISBN 978-1-60260-827-6

Published by Barbour Publishing, Inc., P.O. Box 719,
Uhrichsville, Ohio 44683, www.barbourbooks.com

*Our mission is to publish and distribute inspirational
products offering exceptional value and biblical
encouragement to the masses.*

ecpa Member of the
Evangelical Christian
Publishers Association

Printed in the United States of America.

CONTENTS

LOVE FROM
THE FATHER

Warm Our Hearts
with Thy Love

*O*h God, who made the summer
and warmed the earth with beauty,
Warm our hearts with gratitude
and devotion to our duty.
For in this age of violence, rebellion, and defiance,
We've forgotten the true meaning
of dependable reliance.
We have lost our sense of duty
and our sense of values, too,
And what was once unsanctioned no longer is taboo.
Our standards have been lowered,
and we resist all discipline,
And our vision has been narrowed
and blinded to all sin.
Oh, put the summer brightness
in our closed, unseeing eyes,
So in the careworn faces that we pass we'll recognize
The heartbreak and the loneliness,
the trouble and despair
That a word of understanding
would make easier to bear.
Oh God, look down on our cold hearts
and warm them with Your love,
And grant us Your forgiveness
which we're so unworthy of.

The Hand of God
Is Everywhere

*I*t's true we have never looked on His face,
But His likeness shines forth from every place,
For the hand of God is everywhere
Along life's busy thoroughfare,
And His presence can be felt and seen
Right in the midst of our daily routine.
Things we touch and see and feel
Are what make God so very real.

GOD'S LOVE IS A HAVEN IN
THE STORMS OF LIFE

God's love is like an island
in life's ocean, vast and wide,
A peaceful, quiet shelter from the restless, rising tide.
God's love is like a fortress,
and we seek protection there
When the waves of tribulation
seem to drown us in despair.
God's love is like a sanctuary
where our souls can find sweet rest
From the struggle and the tension
of life's fast and futile quest.
God's love is like a tower rising far above the crowd,
And God's smile is like the sunshine
breaking through the threatening cloud.
God's love is like a beacon
burning bright with faith and prayer,
And through all the changing scenes of life
we can find a haven there.

WHERE THERE IS LOVE

*W*here there is love the heart is light,
Where there is love the day is bright.
Where there is love there is a song
To help when things are going wrong.
Where there is love there is a smile
To make all things seem more worthwhile.
Where there is love there's a quiet peace,
A tranquil place where turmoils cease.
Love changes darkness into light
And makes the heart take wingless flight.
Oh, blessed are those who walk in love
They also walk with God above. . . .
And love that once seemed yours alone
God gently blends into His own.

Worry No More—
God Knows the Score

Have you ever been caught in a web you didn't weave,
Involved in conditions that are hard to believe?
Have you ever felt you must speak and explain and deny
A story that's groundless or a small, whispered lie?
Have you ever heard rumors you would like to refute
Or some telltale gossip you would like to dispute?
Well, don't be upset, for God knows the score,
And with God as your judge you need worry no more.
For men may misjudge you, but God's verdict is fair,
For He looks deep inside and is deeply aware
Of every small detail in your pattern of living,
And always He's fair and lenient and forgiving,
And knowing that God is your judge and your jury
Frees you completely from man's falseness and fury.
And secure in this knowledge, let your thoughts rise above
Man's small, shallow judgments that are so empty of
God's goodness and greatness in judging men,
And forget ugly rumors and be happy again.

How Great the Yield
from a Fertile Field

The farmer plows through the fields of green,
And the blade of the plow is sharp and keen,
But the seed must be sown to bring forth grain,
For nothing is born without suffering and pain,
And God never plows in the soul of man
Without intention and purpose and plan.
So whenever you feel the plow's sharp blade,
Let not your heart be sorely afraid,
For like the farmer, God chooses a field
From which He expects an excellent yield.
So rejoice though your heart be broken in two—
God seeks to bring forth a rich harvest in you.

GOD LOVES US

We are all God's children and He loves us, every one.
He freely and completely forgives
all that we have done,
Asking only if we're ready to follow where He leads,
Content that in His wisdom
He will answer all our needs.

FAITH AND TRUST

*S*ometimes, when a light
goes out of our lives,
and we are left in darkness
and we do not know which way to go,
we must put our hand
into the hand of God
and ask Him to lead us;
and if we let our lives become a prayer
until we are strong enough
to stand under the weight
of our own thoughts again,
somehow, even the most difficult
hours are bearable.

FORTRESS OF FAITH

It's easy to say "In God we trust"
when life is radiant and fair,
But the test of faith is only found
when there are burdens to bear.
For our claim to faith in the sunshine
is really no faith at all,
For when roads are smooth and days are bright
our need for God is so small.
And no one discovers the fullness
or the greatness of God's love
Unless they have walked in the darkness
with only a light from above.
For the faith to endure whatever comes
is born of sorrow and trials
And strengthened only by discipline
and nurtured by self-denials.
So be not disheartened by troubles,
for trials are the building blocks
On which to erect a fortress of faith,
secure on God's ageless rocks.

Do Not Be Anxious

Do not be anxious, said our Lord,
Have peace from day to day—
The lilies neither toil nor spin,
Yet none are clothed as they.
The meadowlark with sweetest song
Fears not for bread or nest
Because he trusts our Father's love,
And God knows what is best.

NEVER BE DISCOURAGED

There is really nothing we need know
or even try to understand
If we refuse to be discouraged
and trust God's guiding hand,
So take heart and meet each minute
with faith in God's great love,
Aware that every day of life
is controlled by God above.
And never dread tomorrow
or what the future brings.
Just pray for strength and courage
and trust God in all things,
And never grow discouraged—
be patient and just wait,
For God never comes too early,
and He never comes too late.

God's Hand Is
Always There

I am perplexed and often vexed,
And sometimes I cry and sadly sigh,
But do not think, dear Father above,
That I question You or Your unfailing love.
It's just that sometimes when I reach out,
You seem to be nowhere about.
And while I'm sure You love me still,
I know in my heart that You always will,
Somehow I feel I cannot reach You.
And though I get on my knees and beseech You,
I cannot bring You close to me,
And I feel adrift on life's raging sea.
But though I cannot find your hand
To lead me on to the promised land,
I still believe with all my being
Your hand is there beyond my seeing.

TRUST GOD

Take heart and meet each minute
with faith in God's great love,
Aware that every day of life
is controlled by God above.
And never dread tomorrow
or what the future brings—
Just pray for strength and courage
and trust God in all things.

The Joy of Living

Expectation! Anticipation! Realization!

God gives us a power we so seldom employ,
For we're so unaware it is filled with such joy.
The gift that God gives us is anticipation,
Which we can fulfill with sincere expectation,
For there's power in belief when we think we will find
Joy for the heart and peace for the mind,
And believing the day will bring a surprise
Is not only pleasant but surprisingly wise.
For we open the door to let joy walk through
When we learn to expect the best, and the most, too,
And believing we'll find a happy surprise
Makes reality out of a fancied surmise.

Wish Not for Ease or to Do as You Please

If wishes worked like magic
and plans worked that way, too,
And if everything you wished for,
whether good or bad for you,
Immediately were granted
with no effort on your part,
You'd experience no fulfillment
of your spirit or your heart.
For things achieved too easily
lose their charm and meaning, too,
For it is life's difficulties
and the trial times we go through
That make us strong in spirit
and endow us with the will
To surmount the insurmountable
and to climb the highest hill.
So wish not for the easy way
to win your heart's desire,
For the joy's in overcoming
and withstanding flood and fire,
For to triumph over trouble
and grow stronger with defeat
Is to win the kind of victory
that will make your life complete.

WEALTH

Good health, good humor,
And good sense,
No one is poor
With this defense.

MEMORIES

Tender little memories
Of some word or deed
Give us strength and courage
When we are in need.
Blessed little memories
Help us bear the cross
And soften all the bitterness
Of failure and loss.
Precious little memories
Of little things we've done
Make the very darkest day
A bright and happy one.

GIVING IS THE KEY
TO LIVING

*E*very day is a reason for giving
And giving is the key to living.
So let us give ourselves away,
Not just today but every day,
And remember, a kind and thoughtful deed
Or a hand outstretched in a time of need
Is the rarest of gifts, for it is a part,
Not of the purse but of a loving heart.
And he who gives of himself will find
True joy of heart and peace of mind.

LIFE

A little laughter, a little song,
A little teardrop
When things go wrong,
A little calm
And a little strife
A little loving
And that is life.

BE OF GOOD CHEER—
THERE'S NOTHING TO FEAR

Cheerful thoughts like sunbeams
lighten up the darkest fears,
For when the heart is happy
there's just no time for tears. . . ,
For the nature of our attitudes
toward circumstantial things
Determines our acceptance
of the problems that life brings.
And since fear and dread and worry
cannot help in any way,
It's much healthier and happier
to be cheerful every day.
And if you'll only try it,
you will find, without a doubt,
A cheerful attitude's something
no one should be without,
For when the heart is cheerful,
it cannot be filled with fear,
And without fear, the way ahead
seems more distinct and clear,
And we realize there's nothing
that we must face alone,
For our heavenly Father loves us,
and our problems are His own.

Take Time to Be Kind

Kindness is a virtue given by the Lord;
It pays dividends in happiness, and joy is its reward.
For if you practice kindness in all you say and do,
The Lord will wrap His kindness
around your heart and you.

FINDING FAITH IN A FLOWER

Sometimes when faith is running low
And I cannot fathom why things are so,
I walk among the flowers that grow
And learn the answers to all I would know.
For among my flowers I have come to see
Life's miracle and its mystery,
And standing in silence and reverie,
My faith comes flooding back to me.

MEMORY RENDEZVOUS

Memory builds a little pathway
that goes winding through my heart.
It's a lovely, quiet, gentle trail
from other things apart.
I only meet, when traveling there,
the folks I like the best,
For this road I call remembrance
is hidden from the rest.
But I hope I'll always find you
in my memory rendezvous,
For I keep this little secret place
to meet with folks like you.

STEPPING STONES TO GOD

An aching heart is but a stepping stone
To greater joy than you've ever known,
For things that cause the heart to ache
Until you think that it must break
Become the strength by which we climb
To higher heights that are sublime
And feel the radiance of God's smiles
When we have soared above life's trials.
So when you're overwhelmed with fears
And all your hopes are drenched in tears,
Think not that life has been unfair
And given you too much to bear,
For God has chosen you because,
With all your weaknesses and flaws,
He feels that you are worthy of
The greatness of His wondrous love.

Climb Till Your Dream Comes True

*O*ften your tasks will be many,
and more than you think you can do.
Often the road will be rugged,
and the hills insurmountable, too.
But always remember, the hills ahead
are never as steep as they seem,
And with faith in your heart, start upward
and climb till you reach your dream.
For nothing in life that is worthy
is ever too hard to achieve
If you have the courage to try it
and you have the faith to believe.
For faith is a force that is greater
than knowledge or power or skill,
And many defeats turn to triumphs
if you trust in God's wisdom and will.
For faith is a mover of mountains—
there's nothing that God cannot do—
So start out today with faith in your heart
and climb till your dream comes true.

LOVE DIVINE,
ALL LOVES EXCELLING

In a myriad of miraculous ways
God shapes our lives and changes our days.
Beyond our will or even knowing
God keeps our spirits ever growing.
For lights and shadows, sun and rain,
Sadness and gladness, joy and pain
Combine to make our lives complete
And give us victory through defeat.
Oh "Love divine, all loves excelling,"
In troubled hearts You just keep on dwelling,
Patiently waiting for a prodigal son
To say at last, "Thy will be done."

Peace that Passes Understanding

LIFE'S CROSSROADS

Sometimes we come to life's crossroads
and view what we think is the end,
But God has a much wider vision,
and He knows it's only a bend.
The road will go on and get smoother,
and after we've stopped for a rest,
The path that lies hidden beyond us
is often the part that is best.
So rest and relax and grow stronger
let go and let God share your load,
And have faith in a brighter tomorrow;
you've just come to a bend in the road.

The Peace of Meditation

So we may know God better
and feel His quiet power,
Let us daily keep in silence a meditation hour.
For to understand God's greatness
and to use His gifts each day,
The soul must learn to meet Him in a meditative way.
For our Father tells His children
that if they would know His will
They must seek Him in the silence
when all is calm and still.
For nature's great forces are found in quiet things
Like softly falling snowflakes
drifting down on angels' wings
Or petals dropping soundlessly
from a lovely full-blown rose.
So God comes closest to us
when our souls are in repose.
So let us plan with prayerful care to always allocate
A certain portion of each day to be still and meditate.
For when everything is quiet
and we're lost in meditation,
Our souls are then preparing for a deeper dedication
That will make it wholly possible to quietly endure
The violent world around us,
for in God we are secure.

THE FORTRESS OF
PEACE WITHIN

Peace is not something you fight for
with bombs and missiles that kill.
Peace is attained in the silence
that comes when the heart stands still.
For hearts that are restless and warlike
with longings that never cease
Can never contribute ideas
that bring the world nearer to peace.
For as dew never falls on a morning
that follows a dark, stormy night,
The peace and grace of our Father
fall not on a soul in flight.
So if we seek peace for all people,
there is but one place to begin,
And the armament race will not win it,
for the fortress of peace is within.

REMEMBRANCE ROAD

There's a road I call remembrance
where I walk each day with you.
It's a pleasant, happy road, my dear,
all filled with memories true.
Today it leads me through a spot
where I can dream awhile,
And in its tranquil peacefulness
I touch your hand and smile.
There are hills and fields and budding trees
and stillness that's so sweet
That it seems that this must be the place
where God and humans meet.
I hope we can go back again
and golden hours renew,
And God go with you always, dear,
until the day we do.

LEARN TO REST

We all need short vacations
in life's fast and maddening race
An interlude of quietness
from the constant, jet-age pace,
So when your day is pressure-packed
and your hours are all too few,
Just close your eyes and meditate
and let God talk to you.
For when we keep on pushing,
we're not following in God's way
We are foolish, selfish robots
mechanized to fill each day
With unimportant trivia
that makes life more complex
And gives us greater problems to irritate and vex.
So when your nervous network
becomes a tangled mess,
Just close your eyes in silent prayer
and ask the Lord to bless
Each thought that you are thinking,
each decision you must make,
As well as every word you speak
and every step you take.
For only by the grace of God
can you gain self-control,
And only meditative thoughts
can restore your peace and soul.

THE COMFORT AND SWEETNESS OF PEACE

After the clouds, the sunshine,
After the winter, the spring,
After the shower, the rainbow—
For life is a changeable thing.
After the night, the morning,
Bidding all darkness cease,
After life's cares and sorrows,
The comfort and sweetness of peace.

A PATTERN FOR LIVING

"Love one another as I have loved you"
May seem impossible to do,
But if you will try to trust and believe,
Great are the joys that you will receive.
For love makes us patient, understanding, and kind,
And we judge with our hearts and not with our minds,
For as soon as love entered the heart's open door,
The faults we once saw are not there anymore,
And the things that seem wrong begin to look right
When viewed in the softness of love's gentle light,
For love works in ways that are wondrous and strange,
And there is nothing in life that love cannot change,
And all that God promised will someday come true
When you have loved one another
the way He loved you.

BEAUTY AND PEACE

God in His loving and all-wise way
Makes the heart that was young yesterday
Serene and more gentle and less restless, too,
Content to remember the joys it once knew.
And all that we sought on the pathway of pleasure
Becomes but a memory to cherish and treasure—
The fast pace grows slower and the spirit serene,
And the soul can envision what the eyes have not seen.
And so while life's springtime is sweet to recall,
The autumn of life is the best time of all,
For our wild youthful yearnings all gradually cease,
And God fills our days with beauty and peace!

In Christ All Men May Live Again

*L*et us all remember, when our faith is running low,
Christ is more than just a figure
wrapped in an ethereal glow.
For He came and dwelled among us
and He knows our every need,
And He loves and understands us
and forgives each sinful deed.
He was crucified and buried and rose again in glory,
And the Savior's resurrection
makes the wondrous Easter story
An abiding reassurance that man dies to live again
In a land that's free from trouble
where there's peace among all men.

BLESSINGS DEVISED BY GOD

*G*od speaks to us in many ways,
Altering our lives, our plans, and our days,
And His blessings come in many guises
That He alone in love devises,
And sorrow, which we dread so much,
Can bring a very healing touch.
For when we fail to heed His voice,
We leave the Lord no other choice
Except to use a firm, stern hand
To make us know He's in command.
For on the wings of loss and pain,
The peace we often sought in vain
Will come to us with sweet surprise,
For God is merciful and wise.
And through dark hours of tribulation,
God gives us time for meditation,
And nothing can be counted loss
Which teaches us to bear our cross.

A WORD OF
UNDERSTANDING

May peace and understanding
Give you strength and courage, too,
And may the hours and days ahead
Hold a new hope for you.
For the sorrow that is yours today
Will pass away; and then
You'll find the sun of happiness
Will shine for you again.

"I Am the Light of the World"

In this sick world of hatred and violence and sin,
Where society renounces morals
and rejects discipline,
We stumble in darkness groping vainly for light
To distinguish the difference
between wrong and right.
But dawn cannot follow this night of despair
Unless faith lights a candle in all hearts everywhere.
And warmed by the glow, our hate melts away
And love lights the path to a peaceful new day.

He Asks so Little and Gives so Much

What must I do to ensure peace of mind?
Is the answer I'm seeking too hard to find?
How can I know what God wants me to be?
How can I tell what's expected of me?
Where can I go for guidance and aid
To help me correct the errors I've made?
The answer is found in doing three things,
And great is the gladness that doing them brings.
"Do justice"—"Love kindness"—
"Walk humbly with God"—
For with these three things as your rule and your rod,
All things worth having are yours to achieve,
If you follow God's words and have faith to believe.

GIFTS OF FRIENDSHIP

THE GOLDEN CHAIN
OF FRIENDSHIP

Friendship is a golden chain,
the links are friends so dear,
And like a rare and precious jewel,
it's treasured more each year.
It's clasped together firmly
with a love that's deep and true,
And it's rich with happy memories
and fond recollections, too.
Time can't destroy its beauty,
for as long as memory lives,
Years can't erase the pleasure
that the joy of friendship gives.
For friendship is a priceless gift
that can't be bought or sold,
And to have an understanding friend
is worth far more than gold.
And the golden chain of friendship
is a strong and blessed tie
Binding kindred hearts together
as the years go passing by.

HEART GIFTS

It's not the things that can be bought
That are life's richest treasures,
It's just the little "heart gifts"
That money cannot measure.
A cheerful smile, a friendly word,
A sympathetic nod,
Are priceless little treasures
From the storehouse of our God.
They are the things that can't be bought
With silver or with gold,
For thoughtfulness and kindness
And love are never sold.
They are the priceless things in life
For which no one can pay,
And the giver finds rich recompense
In giving them away.

STRANGERS ARE FRIENDS WE HAVEN'T MET

God knows no strangers, He loves us all,
The poor, the rich, the great, the small.
He is a friend who is always there
To share our troubles and lessen our care.
For no one is a stranger in God's sight,
For God is love, and in His light
May we, too, try in our small way
To make new friends from day to day.
So pass no stranger with an unseeing eye,
For God may be sending a new friend by.

Friends Are Life's Gift of Love

If people like me didn't know people like you,
Life would lose its meaning and its richness, too.
For the friends that we make are life's gift of love,
And I think friends are sent right from heaven above.
And thinking of you somehow makes me feel
That God is love and He's very real.

Discouragement and Dreams

So many things in the line of duty
Drain us of effort and leave us no beauty,
And the dust of the soul grows thick and unswept,
The spirit is drenched in tears unwept.
But just as we fall beside the road,
Discouraged with life and bowed down with our load,
We lift our eyes, and what seemed a dead end
Is the street of dreams where we meet a friend.

THE ART OF GREATNESS

It's not fortune or fame or worldwide acclaim
That makes for true greatness you'll find
It's the wonderful art of teaching the heart
To always be thoughtful and kind!

A Friend Is a
Gift from God

Among the great and glorious gifts
our heavenly Father sends
Is the gift of understanding
that we find in loving friends.
For in this world of trouble
that is filled with anxious care,
Everybody needs a friend
in whom they're free to share
The little secret heartaches
that lay heavy on the mind—
Not just a mere acquaintance
but someone who's just our kind. . . .
So when we need some sympathy
or a friendly hand to touch
Or one who listens tenderly and speaks
words that mean so much,
We seek a true and trusted friend
in the knowledge that we'll find
A heart that's sympathetic
and an understanding mind.
And often just without a word
there seems to be a union
Of thoughts and kindred feelings,
for God gives true friends communion.

LIFE IS A GARDEN

Life is a garden; good friends are the flowers,
And times spent together life's happiest hours.
And friendship, like flowers, blooms ever more fair
When carefully tended by dear friends who care.
And life's lovely garden would be sweeter by far
If all who passed through it were as nice as you are.

Don't Count Your Birthdays by Years

*Time is not measured by the years that you live
But by the deeds that you do and the joy that you give.
And from birthday to birthday, the good Lord above
Bestows on His children the gift of His love,
Asking us only to share it with others
By treating all people not as strangers but brothers.
And each day as it comes brings a chance to each one
To live life to the fullest, leaving nothing undone
That would brighten the life or lighten the load
Of some weary traveler lost on life's road.
So it doesn't matter how long we may live
If as long as we live we unselfishly give.*

The Gift of Friendship

Friendship is a priceless gift
that cannot be bought or sold,
But its value is far greater than
a mountain made of gold—
For gold is cold and lifeless,
it can neither see nor hear,
And in the time of trouble
it is powerless to cheer.
It has no ears to listen,
no heart to understand,
It cannot bring you comfort
or reach out a helping hand—
So when you ask God for a gift
be thankful if He sends
Not diamonds, pearls, or riches,
but the love of real true friends.

To Comfort You

YOU ARE NEVER ALONE

*T*here's truly nothing we need know
If we have faith wherever we go.
God will be there to help us bear
Our disappointments, pain, and care,
For He is our Shepherd, our Father, our Guide.
You're never alone with the Lord at your side.

SOMEBODY CARES

Somebody cares and always will—
The world forgets, but God loves you still.
You cannot go beyond His love
No matter what you're guilty of,
For God forgives until the end.
He is your faithful, loyal friend.
And though you try to hide your face,
There is no shelter anyplace
That can escape His watchful eye,
For on the earth and in the sky
He's ever-present and always there
To take you in His tender care
And bind the wounds and mend the breaks
When all the world around forsakes.
Somebody cares and loves you still,
And God is the Someone who always will.

HE UNDERSTANDS

Although it sometimes seems to us
our prayers have not been heard,
God always knows our every need
without a single word,
And He will not forsake us
even though the way is steep,
For always He is near to us,
a tender watch to keep.
And in good time He will answer us,
and in His love He'll send
Greater things than we have asked
and blessings without end.
So though we do not understand
why trouble comes to man,
Can we not be contented
just to know it is God's plan?

We Can't, but God Can

Why things happen as they do
we do not always know,
And we cannot always fathom
why our spirits sink so low.
We flounder in our dark distress,
we are wavering and unstable,
But when we're most inadequate,
the Lord God's always able—
For though we are incapable,
God's powerful and great,
And there's no darkness of the mind
God cannot penetrate. . . .
And while He may not instantly
unravel all the strands
Of the tangled thoughts that trouble us,
He completely understands—
And in His time, if we have faith,
He will gradually restore
The brightness to our spirits
that we've been longing for.
So remember there's no cloud too dark
for God's light to penetrate
If we keep on believing
and have faith enough to wait.

A Time of Renewal and Spiritual Blessing

No one likes to be sick, and yet we know
It takes sunshine and rain to make flowers grow,
And if we never were sick and we never felt pain,
We'd be like a desert without any rain.
And who wants a life that is barren and dry
With never a cloud to darken the sky?
For continuous sun goes unrecognized
Like the blessings God sends, which are often disguised,
For sometimes a sickness that seems so distressing
Is a time of renewal and spiritual blessing.

LIFE'S DISAPPOINTMENTS ARE GOD'S SWEETEST APPOINTMENTS

Out of life's misery born of man's sins,
A fuller, richer life begins,
For when we are helpless with no place to go
And our hearts are heavy and our spirits are low,
If we place our lives in God's hands
And surrender completely to His will and demands,
The darkness lifts and the sun shines through,
And by His touch we are born anew.
So praise God for trouble that cuts like a knife
And disappointments that shatter your life,
For with patience to wait and faith to endure,
Your life will be blessed and your future secure,
For God is but testing your faith and your love
Before He appoints you to rise far above
All the small things that so sorely distress you,
For God's only intention is to strengthen and bless you.

FAITH FOR DARK DAYS

When dark days come—and they come to us all—
We feel so helpless and lost and small.
We cannot fathom the reason why,
And it is futile for us to try
To find the answer, the reason or cause,
For the master plan is without any flaws.
And when the darkness shuts out the light,
We must lean on faith to restore our sight,
For there is nothing we need know
If we have faith that wherever we go
God will be there to help us to bear
Our disappointments, pain, and care.
For He is our Shepherd, our Father, our Guide,
And you're never alone with the Lord at your side.
So may the great Physician attend you,
And may His healing completely mend you.

PATIENCE

Most of the battles of life are won
By looking beyond the clouds to the sun
And having the patience to wait for the day
When the sun comes out and the clouds float away.

YESTERDAY, TODAY, AND TOMORROW

*Y*esterday's dead, tomorrow's unborn,
So there's nothing to fear and nothing to mourn,
For all that is past and all that has been
Can never return to be lived once again.
And what lies ahead, or the things that will be,
Are still in God's hands, so it is not up to me
To live in the future that is God's great unknown,
For the past and the present God claims for His own.
So all I need do is to live for today
And trust God to show me the truth and the way,
For it's only the memory of things that have been
And expecting tomorrow to bring trouble again
That fills my today, which God wants to bless,
With uncertain fears and borrowed distress.
For all I need live for is this one little minute,
For life's here and now and eternity's in it.

Your Life Will Be Blessed if You Look for the Best

*I*t's easy to grow downhearted
when nothing goes your way,
It's easy to be discouraged
when you have a troublesome day,
But trouble is only a challenge
to spur you on to achieve
The best that God has to offer,
if you have the faith to believe!

MOVER OF MOUNTAINS

Faith is a force that is greater
than knowledge or power or skill,
And the darkest defeat turns to triumph
if you trust in God's wisdom and will,
For faith is a mover of mountains—
there's nothing man cannot achieve
If he has the courage to try it
and then has the faith to believe.

ADVERSITY CAN DISTRESS US OR BLESS US

The way we use adversity is strictly our own choice,
For in God's hands, adversity
can make the heart rejoice.
For everything God sends to us,
no matter in what form,
Is sent with plan and purpose;
for by the fierceness of a storm,
The atmosphere is changed and cleared,
and the earth is washed and clean,
And the high winds of adversity
can make restless souls serene.
And while it's very difficult
for mankind to understand
God's intentions and His purpose
and the workings of His hand,
If we observe the miracles that happen every day,
We cannot help but be convinced
that in His wondrous way
God makes what seemed unbearable
and painful and distressing
Easily acceptable when we view it as a blessing.

THE BEAUTY OF PRAYER

LITTLE SPRINGTIME PRAYER

God, grant this little springtime prayer
And make our hearts, grown cold with care,
Once more aware of the waking earth
Now pregnant with life and bursting with birth.
For how can man feel any fear or doubt
When on every side all around and about
The March winds blow across man's face
And whisper of God's power and grace?
Oh, give us faith to believe again
That peace on earth, goodwill to men
Will follow this winter of man's mind
And awaken his heart and make him kind.
And just as great nature sends the spring
To give new birth to each sleeping thing,
God, grant rebirth to man's slumbering soul
And help him forsake his selfish goal.

MORE OF THEE, LESS OF ME

Take me and break me and make me, dear God,
just what You want me to be.
Give me the strength to accept what You send
and eyes with the vision to see
All the small, arrogant ways that I have
and the vain little things that I do.
Make me aware that I'm often concerned
more with myself than with You.
Uncover before me my weakness and greed
and help me to search deep inside
So I may discover how easy it is
to be selfishly lost in my pride.
And then in Thy goodness and mercy,
look down on this weak, erring one
And tell me that I am forgiven
for all I've so willfully done,
And teach me to humbly start following
the path that the dear Savior trod
So I'll find at the end of life's journey
a home in the city of God.

LISTEN IN THE QUIETNESS

To try to run away from life
is impossible to do,
For no matter where you chance to go,
your troubles will follow you;
For though the scenery is different,
when you look deep inside you'll find
The same deep, restless longings
that you thought you left behind.
So when life becomes a problem
much too great for us to bear,
Instead of trying to escape,
let us withdraw in prayer.
For withdrawal means renewal
if we withdraw to pray
And listen in the quietness
to hear what God will say.

A Prayer for
Peace and Patience

God, teach me to be patient, teach me to go slow.
Teach me how to wait on You
when my way I do not know.
Teach me sweet forbearance,
when things do not go right,
So I remain unruffled when others grow uptight.
Teach me how to quiet my racing, rising heart,
So I might hear the answer You are trying to impart.
Teach me to let go, dear God,
and pray undisturbed until
My heart is filled with inner peace
and I learn to know Your will.

Now I Lay Me Down to Sleep

I remember so well this prayer I said
Each night as my mother tucked me in bed,
And today this same prayer is still the best way
To sign off with God at the end of the day
And to ask Him your soul to safely keep
As you wearily close your tired eyes in sleep,
Feeling content that the Father above
Will hold you secure in His great arms of love.
And having His promise, that if ere you wake
His angels reach down, your sweet soul to take,
Is perfect assurance that, awake or asleep,
God is always right there to tenderly keep
All of His children ever safe in His care,
For God's here and He's there and He's everywhere.
So into His hands each night as I sleep
I commend my soul for the dear Lord to keep,
Knowing that if my soul should take flight
It will soar to the land where there is no night.

My Garden of Prayer

My garden beautifies my yard
and adds fragrance to the air,
But it is also my cathedral
and my quiet place of prayer.
So little do we realize
that the glory and the power
Of Him who made the universe
lies hidden in a flower!

I Come to Meet You

I come to meet You, God, and as I linger here
I seem to feel You very near.
A rustling leaf, a rolling slope
Speak to my heart of endless hope.
The sun just rising in the sky,
The waking birdlings as they fly,
The grass all wet with morning dew
Are telling me I just met You.
And gently thus the day is born
As night gives way to breaking morn,
And once again I've met You, God,
And worshipped on Your holy sod.
For who could see the dawn break through
Without a glimpse of heaven and You?
For who but God could make the day
And softly put the night away?

WIDEN MY VISION

God, open my eyes so I may see
And feel Your presence close to me.
Give me strength for my stumbling feet
As I battle the crowd on life's busy street,
And widen the vision of my unseeing eyes
So in passing faces I'll recognize
Not just a stranger, unloved and unknown,
But a friend with a heart that is much like my own.
Give me perception to make me aware
That scattered profusely on life's thoroughfare
Are the best gifts of God that we daily pass by
As we look at the world with an unseeing eye.

MAKE YOUR DAY BRIGHT
BY THINKING RIGHT

*D*on't start your day by supposin'
that trouble is just ahead.
It's better to stop supposin'
and start with a prayer instead.
And make it a prayer of thanksgiving
for the wonderful things God has wrought,
Like the beautiful sunrise and sunset—
God's gifts that are free and not bought.
For what is the use of supposin'
that dire things could happen to you,
Worrying about some misfortune
that seldom if ever comes true.
But instead of just idle supposin',
step forward to meet each new day
Secure in the knowledge God's near you
to lead you each step of the way.
For supposin' the worst things will happen
only helps to make them come true,
And you darken the bright, happy moments
that the dear Lord has given to you.
So if you desire to be happy
and get rid of the misery of dread,
Just give up supposin' the worst things
and look for the best things instead.

Make Me a Channel of Blessing Today

*M*ake me a channel of blessing today,
I ask again and again when I pray.
Do I turn a deaf ear to the Master's voice
or refuse to hear His direction and choice?
I only know at the end of the day
that I did so little to pay my way.

No Favor Do
I Seek Today

I come not to ask, to plead, or implore You;
I just come to tell You how much I adore You.
For to kneel in Your presence makes me feel blessed,
For I know that You know all my needs best.
And it fills me with joy just to linger with You,
As my soul You replenish and my heart You renew.
For prayer is much more than just asking for things;
It's the peace and contentment that quietness brings.
So thank You again for Your mercy and love
And for making me heir to Your kingdom above.

SHOW ME THE WAY

Show me the way, not to fortune and fame,
Not how to win laurels or praise for my name,
But show me the way to spread the great story
That Thine is the kingdom and power and glory.

DAILY PRAYERS ARE
HEAVEN'S STAIRS

The stairway rises heaven-high, the steps are dark and steep.
In weariness we climb them as we stumble, fall, and weep.
And many times we falter along the path of prayer,
Wondering if You hear us and if You really care.
Oh, give us some assurance; restore our faith anew,
So we can keep on climbing the stairs of prayer to You.
For we are weak and wavering, uncertain and unsure,
And only meeting You in prayer can help us to endure
All life's trials and troubles, its sickness, pain, and sorrow,
And give us strength and courage
to face and meet tomorrow.

My Daily Prayer

God, be my resting place and my protection
In hours of trouble, defeat, and dejection.
May I never give away to self-pity and sorrow,
May I always be sure of a better tomorrow,
May I stand undaunted come what may,
Secure in the knowledge I have only to pray
And ask my Creator and Father above
To keep me serene in His grace and His love.

ANXIOUS PRAYERS

*W*hen we are deeply disturbed by a problem
and our minds are filled with doubt,
And we struggle to find a solution,
but there seems to be no way out,
We futilely keep on trying
to untangle our web of distress,
But our own little, puny efforts
meet with very little success.
And finally, exhausted and weary,
discouraged and downcast and low,
With no foreseeable answer
and with no other place to go,
We kneel down in sheer desperation
and slowly and stumblingly pray,
Then impatiently wait for an answer
which we fully expect right away. . . .
But God can't get through to the anxious,
who are much too impatient to wait,
You have to believe in God's promise
that He comes not too soon or too late. . . .
So be not impatient or hasty,
just trust in the Lord and believe,
For whatever you ask in faith and love,
in abundance you are sure to receive.

TRUE HAPPINESS

There's Always a Springtime

After the winter comes the spring
To show us again that in everything
There's always a renewal divinely planned,
Flawlessly perfect, the work of God's hand.
And just like the seasons that come and go
When the flowers of spring lay buried in snow,
God sends to the heart in its winter of sadness
A springtime awakening of new hope and gladness.

GREATNESS

A man may be wealthy,
Good fortune may be his fate,
But only man's motives
Can make him truly great.

LOOK ON THE SUNNY SIDE

There are always two sides, the good and the bad,
The dark and the light, the sad and the glad.
But in looking back over the good and the bad,
We're aware of the number of good things we've had,
And in counting our blessings, we find when we're through
We've no reason at all to complain or be blue.
So thank God for the good things He has already done,
And be grateful to Him for the battles you've won
And know that the same God who helped you before
Is ready and willing to help you once more.
Then with faith in your heart, reach out for God's hand
And accept what He sends, though you can't understand.
For our Father in heaven always knows what is best,
And if you trust His wisdom, your life will be blessed.
For always remember that whatever betide you,
You are never alone, for God is beside you.

Brighten the Corner
Where You Are

*W*e cannot all be famous or listed in Who's Who,
But every person, great or small,
has important work to do. . . .
For it's not the big celebrity
in a world of fame and praise,
But it's doing unpretentiously,
in undistinguished ways,
The work that God assigned to us,
unimportant as it seems,
That makes our task outstanding
and brings reality to dreams. . . .
At the spot God placed you, begin at once to do
Little things to brighten up the lives surrounding you.
For if everybody brightened up
the spot on which they're standing
By being more considerate
and a little less demanding,
This dark old world would very soon
eclipse the evening star
If everybody brightened up the corner where they are.

It's a Wonderful World

In spite of the fact we complain and lament
And view this old world with much discontent,
Deploring conditions and grumbling because
There's so much injustice and so many flaws,
It's a wonderful world, and it's people like you
Who make it that way by the things that they do.
For a warm, ready smile or a kind, thoughtful deed
Or a hand outstretched in an hour of need
Can change our whole outlook
and make the world bright
Where a minute before just nothing seemed right.
It's a wonderful world and it always will be
If we keep our eyes open and focused to see
The wonderful things we are capable of
When we open our hearts to God and His love.

GIVE LAVISHLY!
LIVE ABUNDANTLY!

The more you give, the more you get.
The more you laugh, the less you fret.
The more you do unselfishly,
The more you live abundantly.
The more of everything you share,
The more you'll always have to spare.
The more you love, the more you'll find
That life is good and friends are kind,
For only what we give away
Enriches us from day to day.

HAPPINESS

Across the years, we've met in dreams
And shared each other's hopes and schemes.
We've known a friendship rich and rare
And beautiful beyond compare.
But you reached out your arms for more
To catch what you were yearning for,
But little did you think or guess
That one can't capture happiness
Because it's unrestrained and free,
Unfettered by reality.

FLOWERS LEAVE THEIR FRAGRANCE ON THE HAND THAT BESTOWS THEM

There's an old Chinese proverb that if practiced each day
Would change the whole world in a wonderful way.
Its truth is so simple, it's easy to do,
And it works every time and successfully, too.
For you can't do a kindness without a reward
Not in silver nor gold but in joy from the Lord.
You can't light a candle to show others the way
Without feeling the warmth of that bright little ray,
And you can't pluck a rose all fragrant with dew
Without part of its fragrance remaining with you.

His Footsteps

When someone does a kindness,
It always seems to me
That's the way God up in heaven
Would like us all to be.
For when we bring some pleasure
To another human heart,
We have followed in His footsteps
And we've had a little part
In serving God who loves us
For I'm very sure it's true
That in serving those around us,
We serve and please God, too.

TRAVELING TO HEAVEN

Life is a highway on which the years go by,
Sometimes the road is level, sometimes the hills are high.
But as we travel onward to a future that's unknown,
We can make each mile we travel
a heavenly stepping stone!

DEEP IN MY HEART

Happy little memories
go flitting through my mind,
And in all my thoughts and memories
I always seem to find
The picture of your face, dear,
the memory of your touch,
And all the other little things
I've come to love so much.
You cannot go beyond my thoughts
or leave my love behind,
Because I keep you in my heart
and forever on my mind.
And though I may not tell you,
I think you know it's true,
That I find daily happiness in
the very thought of you.

BE GLAD

Be glad that your life has been full and complete,
Be glad that you've tasted the bitter and sweet.
Be glad that you've walked in sunshine and rain,
Be glad that you've felt both pleasure and pain.
Be glad that you've had such a full, happy life,
Be glad for your joy as well as your strife.
Be glad that you've walked with courage each day,
Be glad you've had strength for each step of the way.
Be glad for the comfort that you've found in prayer.
Be glad for God's blessings, His love, and His care.

BLESSINGS OF FAMILY

THE MAGIC OF LOVE

*L*ove is like magic and it always will be,
For love still remains life's sweet mystery.
Love works in ways that are wondrous and strange,
And there's nothing in life that love cannot change.
Love can transform the most commonplace
Into beauty and splendor and sweetness and grace.
Love is unselfish, understanding, and kind,
For it sees with its heart and not with its mind.
Love gives and forgives; there is nothing too much
For love to heal with its magic touch.
Love is the language that every heart speaks,
For love is the one thing that every heart seeks.
And where there is love God, too, will abide
And bless the family residing inside.

What Is Marriage?

Marriage is the union of two people in love,
And love is sheer magic, for it's woven of
Gossamer dreams, enchantingly real,
That people in love are privileged to feel.
But the exquisite ecstasy that captures the heart
Of two people in love is just a small part
Of the beauty and wonder and miracle of
That growth and fulfillment and evolvement of love.
For only long years of living together
And caring and sharing in all kinds of weather
Both pleasure and pain, the glad and the sad,
Teardrops and laughter, the good and the bad
Can add new dimensions and lift love above
The rapturous ecstasies of falling in love.
For ecstasy passes, but it is replaced
By something much greater that cannot be defaced,
For what was in part has now become whole,
For on the wings of the flesh, love entered the soul.

A Gift of Life

A baby is a gift of life
born of the wonder of love—
A little bit of eternity
sent from the Father above,
Giving a new dimension to the love
between husband and wife
And putting an added new meaning
to the wonder and mystery of life.

To My Sister

If I knew the place where wishes come true,
That's where I would go for my wish for you,
And I'd wish you all that you're wishing for,
For no sister on earth deserves it more.
But trials and troubles come to us all,
For that's the way we grow heaven-tall.
And my birthday prayer to our Father above
Is to keep you safe in His infinite love,
And we both know that gifts don't mean much
Compared to our love and God's blessed touch.

For the New Bride

And now you're Mrs. instead of Miss,
And you've sealed your wedding vows with a kiss.
Your future lies in your hands, my dear,
For it's yours to mold from year to year.
God grant that you make it a beautiful thing,
With all of the blessings that marriage can bring.
May you and that fine, lucky man of your choice
Find daily new blessings to make you rejoice,
And year after year may you grow on together
Always finding a rainbow regardless of weather.
And when youthful charms have faded away,
May you look back with joy to your glad wedding day
And thank God for helping to make you a wife
Who discovered the blessings of a full, married life.

MOTHERS ARE
SPECIAL PEOPLE

Mothers are special people
In a million different ways,
And merit loving compliments
And many words of praise,
For a mother's aspiration
Is for her family's success,
To make the family proud of her
And bring them happiness.
And like our heavenly Father,
She's a patient, loving guide,
Someone we can count on
To be always on our side.

It's So Nice to Have a Dad Around the House

Dads are special people—
no home should be without—
For every family will agree
they're so nice to have about.
They are a happy mixture of a small boy and a man,
And they're very necessary in every family plan.
Sometimes they're most demanding
and stern and firm and tough,
But underneath they're soft as silk,
for this is just a bluff.
But in any kind of trouble Dad reaches out his hand,
And you can always count on him
to help and understand.
And while we do not praise Dad
as often as we should,
We love him and admire him,
and while that's understood,
It's only fair to emphasize
his importance and his worth,
For if there were no loving dads,
this would be a loveless earth.

To My Husband

In my eyes there lies no vision
But the sight of your dear face.
In my heart there is no feeling
But the warmth of your embrace.
In my mind there are no thoughts
But the thoughts of you, my dear.
In my soul no other longing
But just to have you near.
All my dreams were built around you
And I've come to know it's true,
In my life there is no living
That is not a part of you.

MOTHERHOOD

The dearest gifts that heaven holds,
the very finest, too,
Were made into one pattern
that was perfect, sweet, and true.
The angels smiled, well pleased, and said,
"Compared to all the others,
This pattern is so wonderful,
let's use it just for mothers!"
And through the years, a mother has
been all that's sweet and good,
For there's a bit of God and love
in all true motherhood.

Love's Priceless Reward

With faith in each other and faith in the Lord
May your marriage be blessed
with love's priceless reward.
For love that endures and makes life worth living
Is built on strong faith and unselfish giving.
So have faith, and the Lord
will guide both of you through
The glorious new life that is waiting for you.

WHAT IS A MOTHER?

It takes a mother's love to make a house a home—
A place to be remembered no matter where we roam.
It takes a mother's patience to bring a child up right
And her courage and her cheerfulness
to make a dark day bright.
It takes a mother's thoughtfulness
to mend the heart's deep hurts
And her skill and her endurance
to mend little socks and shirts.
It takes a mother's kindness to forgive us when we err,
To sympathize in trouble,
and to bow her head in prayer.
It takes a mother's wisdom to recognize our needs
And to give us reassurance by
her loving words and deeds.

THE INSPIRATION OF CREATION

THIS IS MY FATHER'S WORLD

*E*verywhere across the land
You see God's face and touch His hand
Each time you look up in the sky
Or watch the fluffy clouds drift by,
Or feel the sunshine, warm and bright,
Or watch the dark night turn to light,
Or hear a bluebird brightly sing,
Or see the winter turn to spring,
Or stop to pick a daffodil,
Or gather violets on some hill,
Or touch a leaf or see a tree,
It's all God whispering, "This is Me.
And I am faith and I am light
And in Me there shall be no night."

I Meet God in
the Morning

*E*ach day at dawning I lift my heart high
And raise up my eyes to the infinite sky.
I watch the night vanish as a new day is born,
And I hear the birds sing on the wings of the morn.
I see the dew glisten in crystal-like splendor
While God, with a touch that is gentle and tender,
Wraps up in the night and softly tucks it away
And hangs out the sun to herald a new day.
And so I give thanks and my heart kneels to pray,
"God, keep me and guide me and go with me today."

THE MASTERPIECE

Framed by the vast, unlimited sky,
Bordered by mighty waters,
Sheltered by beautiful woodland groves,
Scented with flowers that bloom and die,
Protected by giant mountain peaks—
The land of the great unknown—
Snowcapped and towering, a nameless place
That beckons man on as the gold he seeks,
Bubbling with life and earthly joys,
Reeking with pain and mortal strife,
Dotted with wealth and material gains,
Built on ideals of girls and boys,
Streaked with toil, opportunity's banner unfurled
Stands out the masterpiece of art
Painted by the one great God,
A picture of the world.

GOD IS REAL

I've never seen God, but I know how I feel;
It's people like you who make Him so real.
My God is no stranger—He's so friendly each day,
And He doesn't ask me to weep when I pray.
It seems that I pass Him so often each day
In the faces of people I meet on my way.
He's the stars in the heavens, a smile on some face,
A leaf on a tree or a rose in a vase.
He's winter and autumn and summer and spring
In short, God is every real, wonderful thing.
I wish I might meet Him much more than I do;
I wish there were more people like you.

THE HEAVENS DECLARE
THE GLORY OF GOD

You ask me how I know it's true
that there is a living God.
A God who rules the universe—
the sky, the sea, the sod—
A God who holds all creatures
in the hollow of His hand,
A God who put infinity in one tiny grain of sand,
A God who made the seasons—
winter, summer, fall, and spring—
And put His flawless rhythm into each created thing,
A God who hangs the sun out slowly
with the break of day
And gently takes the stars in and puts the night away,
A God whose mighty handiwork defies the skill of man,
For no architect can alter God's perfect master plan.
What better answers are there to prove His holy being
Than the wonders all around us
that are ours just for the seeing.

ALL NATURE PROCLAIMS
ETERNAL LIFE

Flowers sleeping 'neath the snow,
Awakening when the spring winds blow,
Leafless trees so bare before
Gowned in lacy green once more,
Hard, unyielding, frozen sod
Now softly carpeted by God,
Still streams melting in the spring,
Rippling over rocks that sing,
Barren, windswept, lonely hills
Turning gold with daffodils—
These miracles are all around
Within our sight and touch and sound,
As true and wonderful today
As when the stone was rolled away,
Proclaiming to all doubting men
That in God all things live again.

April

April comes with cheeks a-glowing
Silver streams are all a-flowing,
Flowers open wide their eyes
In lovely rapturous surprise.
Lilies dream beside the brooks,
Violets in meadow nooks,
And the birds gone wild with glee
Fill the woods with melody.

A RAINBOW OF HOPE

The rainbow is God's promise
of hope for you and me,
And though the clouds hang heavy
and the sun we cannot see,
We know above the dark clouds
that fill the stormy sky
Hope's rainbow will come shining through
when the clouds have drifted by.

AFTER THE WINTER
GOD SENDS THE SPRING

*S*pringtime is a season of hope and joy and cheer—
There's beauty all around us to see and touch and hear.
So no matter how downhearted
and discouraged we may be,
New hope is born when we behold
leaves budding on a tree
Or when we see a timid flower
push through the frozen sod
And open wide in glad surprise
its petaled eyes to God.
For this is just God saying, "Lift up your eyes to Me,
And the bleakness of your spirit,
like the budding springtime tree,
Will lose its wintry darkness
and your heavy heart will sing."
For God never sends the winter
without the joy of spring.

My God Is No Stranger

God is no stranger in a faraway place
He's as close as the wind that blows 'cross my face.
It's true I can't see the wind as it blows,
But I feel it around me and my heart surely knows
That God's mighty hand can be felt everywhere,
For there's nothing on earth that is not in God's care.
The sky and the stars, the waves and the sea,
The dew on the grass, the leaves on a tree
Are constant reminders of God and His nearness
Proclaiming His presence with crystal-like clearness.
So how could I think God was far, far away
When I feel Him beside me every hour of the day?
And I've plenty of reasons to know God's my friend,
And this is one friendship that time cannot end.

In God's Tomorrow There Is Eternal Spring

All nature heeds the call of spring
As God awakens everything,
And all that seemed so dead and still
Experiences a sudden thrill
As springtime lays a magic hand
Across God's vast and fertile land.
Oh, the joy in standing by
To watch a sapphire springtime sky
Or see a fragile flower break through
What just a day ago or two
Seemed barren ground still hard with frost,
For in God's world, no life is lost,
And flowers sleep beneath the ground,
But when they hear spring's waking sound,
They push themselves through layers of clay
To reach the sunlight of God's day.
And man and woman, like flowers, too, must sleep
Until called from the darkened deep
To live in that place where angels sing
And where there is eternal spring.

FULFILLMENT

Apple blossoms bursting wide now beautify a tree
And make a springtime picture that is beautiful to see.
Oh fragrant, lovely blossoms,
you'll make a bright bouquet
If I but break your branches
from the apple tree today,
But if I but break your branches
and make your beauty mine,
You'll bear no fruit in season
when severed from the vine,
And when we cut ourselves away
from guidance that's divine,
Our lives will be as fruitless as
the branch without the vine.
For as the flowering branches depend upon the tree
To nourish and fulfill them till they reach futurity,
We, too, must be dependent on our Father up above,
For we are but the branches, and He's the tree of love.

LISTEN IN SILENCE IF
YOU WOULD HEAR

Silently the green leaves grow,
In silence falls the soft, white snow,
Silently the flowers bloom,
In silence sunshine fills a room.
Silently bright stars appear,
In silence velvet night draws near,
And silently God enters in
To free a troubled heart from sin.

GIVING THANKS

FOREVER THANKS

Give thanks for the blessings that daily are ours—
The warmth of the sun, the fragrance of flowers.
With thanks for all the thoughtful,
caring things you always do
And a loving wish for happiness
today and all year through!

A Heart Full of Thanksgiving

*Everyone needs someone to be thankful for,
And each day of life we are aware of this more,
For the joy of enjoying and the fullness of living
Are found only in hearts
that are filled with thanksgiving.*

THINGS TO BE
THANKFUL FOR

The good, green earth beneath our feet,
The air we breathe, the food we eat,
Some work to do, a goal to win,
A hidden longing deep within
That spurs us on to bigger things
And helps us meet what each day brings—
All these things and many more
Are things we should be thankful for.
And most of all, our thankful prayers
Should rise to God because He cares.

BEYOND OUR ASKING

More than hearts can imagine or minds comprehend,
God's bountiful gifts are ours without end.
We ask for a cupful when the vast sea is ours.
We pick a small rosebud from a garden of flowers.
We reach for a sunbeam, but the sun still abides.
We draw one short breath, but there's air on all sides.
Whatever we ask for falls short of God's giving,
For His greatness exceeds every facet of living,
And always God's ready and eager and willing
To pour out His mercy, completely fulfilling
All of man's needs for peace, joy, and rest,
For God gives His children whatever is best.
Just give Him a chance to open His treasures,
And He'll fill your life with unfathomable pleasures—
Pleasures that never grow worn out and faded
And leave us depleted, disillusioned, and jaded.
For God has a storehouse just filled to the brim
With all that man needs, if we'll only ask Him.

Words Can Say So Little

Today is an occasion
for compliments and praise
And saying many of the things
we don't say other days.
For often through the passing days
we feel deep down inside
Unspoken thoughts of thankfulness
and fond, admiring pride.
But words can say so little
when the heart is overflowing,
And often those we love the most
just have no way of knowing
The many things the heart conceals
and never can impart,
For words seem so inadequate
to express what's in the heart.

So Many Reasons
to Love the Lord

Thank You, God, for little things
that come unexpectedly
To brighten up a dreary day
that dawned so dismally.
Thank You, God, for sending a
happy thought my way
To blot out my depression
on a disappointing day.
Thank You, God, for brushing
the dark clouds from my mind
And leaving only sunshine
and joy of heart behind.
Oh God, the list is endless
of the things to thank You for,
But I take them all for granted
and unconsciously ignore
That everything I think or do,
each movement that I make,
Each measured, rhythmic heartbeat,
each breath of life I take
Is something You have given me
for which there is no way
For me in all my smallness
to in any way repay.

THANK YOU, GOD, FOR EVERYTHING

*T*hank You, God, for everything—
the big things and the small—
For every good gift comes from God,
the Giver of them all,
And all too often we accept,
without any thanks or praise,
The gifts God sends as blessings
each day in many ways.
And so at this time we offer up a prayer
To thank You, God, for giving us
a lot more than our share.
First, thank You for the little things
that often come our way—
The things we take for granted
and don't mention when we pray—
Oh, make us more aware, dear God,
of little daily graces
That come to us with sweet surprise
from never-dreamed-of places. . . .
And help us to remember that
the key to life and living
Is to make each prayer a prayer of thanks
and every day Thanksgiving.

A Thankful Heart

Take nothing for granted, for whenever you do,
The joy of enjoying is lessened for you.
For we rob our own lives much more than we know
When we fail to respond or in any way show
Our thanks for the blessings that daily are ours—
The warmth of the sun, the fragrance of flowers,
The beauty of twilight, the freshness of dawn,
The coolness of dew on a green velvet lawn,
The kind little deeds so thoughtfully done,
The favors of friends and the love that someone
Unselfishly gives us in a myriad of ways,
Expecting no payment and no words of praise.
Oh, great is our loss when we no longer find
A thankful response to things of this kind.
For the joy of enjoying and the fullness of living
Are found in the heart that is filled with thanksgiving.

Showers of Blessings

Each day there are showers of blessings
sent from the Father above,
For God is a great, lavish giver,
and there is no end to His love.
And His grace is more than sufficient,
His mercy is boundless and deep,
And His infinite blessings are countless,
and all this we're given to keep
If we but seek God and find Him
and ask for a bounteous measure
Of this wholly immeasurable offering
from God's inexhaustible treasure.
For no matter how big man's dreams are,
God's blessings are infinitely more,
For always God's giving is greater
than what man is asking for.

A SURE WAY TO
A HAPPY DAY

Happiness is something we create in our minds;
It's not something you search for and so seldom find.
It's just waking up and beginning the day
By counting our blessings and kneeling to pray.
It's giving up thoughts that breed discontent
And accepting what comes as a gift heaven-sent.
It's giving up wishing for things we have not
And making the best of whatever we've got.
It's knowing that life is determined for us
And pursuing our tasks without fret, fume, or fuss.
For it's by completing what God gives us to do
That we find real contentment and happiness, too.

A Prayer of Thanks

Thank You, God, for the beauty
around me everywhere,
The gentle rain and glistening dew,
the sunshine and the air,
The joyous gift of feeling
the soul's soft, whispering voice
That speaks to me from deep within
and makes my heart rejoice.

INDEX